Marvelous Manners

The Pirate
Who Said
Please

Timothy Knapman
Illustrated by Jimothy Oliver

QEB Publishing

Pirate Jim is a **pirate king**
who rules the seven seas.

But Jim is very **well behaved**
and never forgets to say
please.

Just one look at his cardboard sword
and all the sharks **shiver** and **shake**.

But he always says,
"**Thank you, Grandma!**"
when she gives him cookies or cake.

His **pirate ship** is a scary sight,
the terror of the living room!

But he remembered to say, "Hey, Mom,
please may I borrow the chair and broom?"

Pirate Jim **loves** a pirate feast—
it's his favorite **pirate treat!**

But he never forgets to ask **nicely**
if he wants some more to eat.

He captures lots of **treasure chests**
without a fuss or a fight.
You see, people give him lots of things...

...because he's so **polite**.

But Pirate Jim **wasn't always nice**
to the rest of his pirate crew.

He was **rude** and **mean** and hosed them down
until they were all soaked through.

He **snatched** whichever toys they brought
before the games had begun.

So the next time they **didn't bring any**,
and the games weren't all that much fun.

At parties he'd forever be shouting,
"Give me more pirate food!"

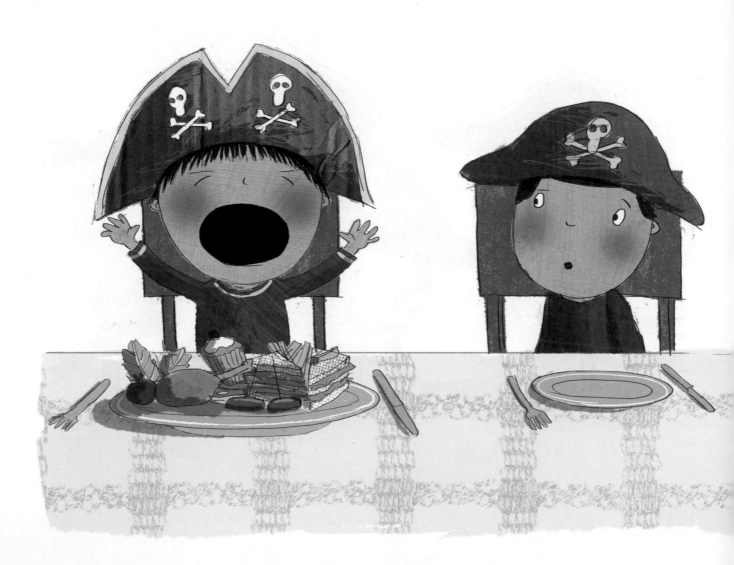

So people stopped inviting him over
and thought this little pirate **rude**.

When he told his crew what to do,
he **wouldn't** say **"please"**–he'd **moan!**

So they left him behind on an island—
faraway and all **alone**.

And that's how **Pirate Jim** was taught
the most important lesson you'll learn:
be **polite** to other people,
and they'll be polite in **return**.

So take note, you salty dogs,
of the tale of **Pirate Jim**.
If you want to be a pirate king,
then you must **behave** like him.

Always say, "**please**" when you're asking
and always **remember to thank**.
Or you'll make the pirates angry,
and you'll have to walk the **plank!**

Next Steps

✠ Ask your child what they know about pirates. Do they know where pirates live or what kind of clothes they wear? Then, look at the first few pages of the book and ask them to describe the pictures on each page.

✠ Ask your child to describe the situations when Jim says, "please" and "thank you." Tell your child that it's important to say "please" if they ask for a favor or would like to have something and to say "thank you" when they are given what they ask for. You could give some examples or do a role-play to illustrate when to say "please" and "thank you."

✠ Ask your child why they think other people give Jim what he wants.

✠ In the past Jim didn't have a lot of fun playing with his friends and probably felt sad that they did not invite him over. His friends even left him alone on an island. Discuss why Jim's friends treated him in this way.

✠ Discuss the picture at the end where Jim and his friends are playing together again. What are the "pirates" in the picture doing and how do they feel? Discuss with your child whether they like to play with friends or play alone. Talk about how being polite makes it more fun to play with others. Ask your child to draw a picture of themselves playing with their friends.

✠ Emphasize that people will treat you the way you treat them. For example, if you are polite to other people, they will be polite to you.

Consultant: Cecilia A. Essau
Editor: Alexandra Koken
Designer: Andrew Crowson

Copyright © QEB Publishing 2012
First published in the United States by
QEB Publishing, Inc.
3 Wrigley, Suite A
Irvine, CA 92618

www.qed-publishing.co.uk

ISBN 978 1 60992 344 0

Printed in China

Library of Congress Cataloging-in-Publication Data

Knapman, Timothy.
The pirate who said please / by Timothy Knapman ; illustrated by Jimothy Rovolio.
   p. cm. -- (Marvelous manners)
 Summary: Cut-throat Jim is a young pirate king who learned the hard way the importance of being courteous.
 ISBN 978-1-60992-266-5 (hardcover, library bound)
 [1. Stories in rhyme. 2. Etiquette--Fiction. 3. Pirates--Fiction.] I. Rovolio, Jimothy, ill. II. Title.
 PZ8.3.K73Pir 2013
 [E]--dc23
                                        2011051877